My First Book About Physics

Donald M. Silver &
Patricia J. Wynne

DOVER PUBLICATIONS, INC.
Mineola, New York

For the best pro team ever at the Works:

Jorge, Alicia, Allison, Angelique, Eli, Gio, Melissa, Wash, and Wendy

What is matter, and what is it made of? How do things move? How does a fox see in the dark? And what makes a rubber duckie float? You'll learn the answers to these and many more questions in this exciting coloring book about physics. Easy-to-understand captions explain the basics of physics in the world around us. Discover how different animals find their food, what causes the tides in the ocean, where light energy comes from, and why a pebble sinks in the water, among other fascinating facts. Plus, you can color each of the realistic illustrations with colored pencils, crayons, or markers.

Bibliographical Note
My First Book About Physics is a new work,
first published by Dover Publications, Inc., in 2019.

International Standard Book Number
ISBN-13: 978-0-486-82614-1
ISBN-10: 0-486-82614-7

Manufactured in the United States by LSC Communications
82614702   2019
www.doverpublications.com

WHAT IT'S ALL ABOUT
Physics is about pushing and pulling, walking and flying, sound and light, and all the things around you. It's about how animals and plants use energy and how people do, too.

LIGHT

SOUND

Moonlight and electric lights help people see at night.

FLYING

A bat makes very high sounds that help it capture a moth to eat.

SOUND

An owl can hear a mouse squeak and pinpoint where it is.

LIGHT

Fireflies blink lights to attract each other.

WALKING

PUSH

Raccoons push on the ground as they walk about at night in search of food.

WALKING

FLYING

SOUND

An earthworm pulls a leaf into its tunnel.

PULL

1

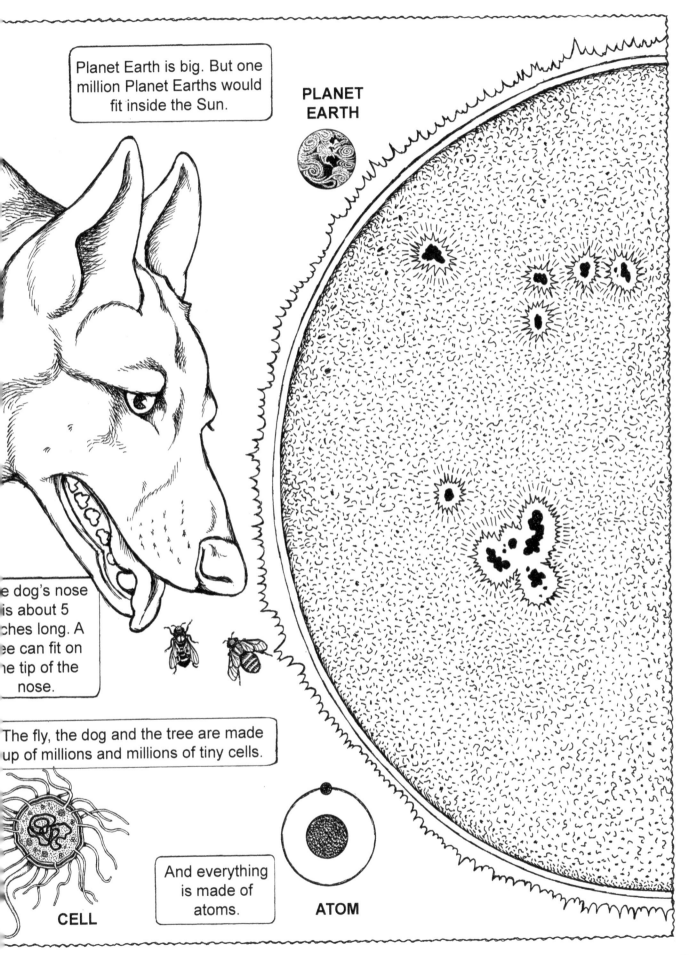

Planet Earth is big. But one million Planet Earths would fit inside the Sun.

PLANET EARTH

e dog's nose is about 5 ches long. A ee can fit on e tip of the nose.

The fly, the dog and the tree are made up of millions and millions of tiny cells.

CELL

And everything is made of atoms.

ATOM

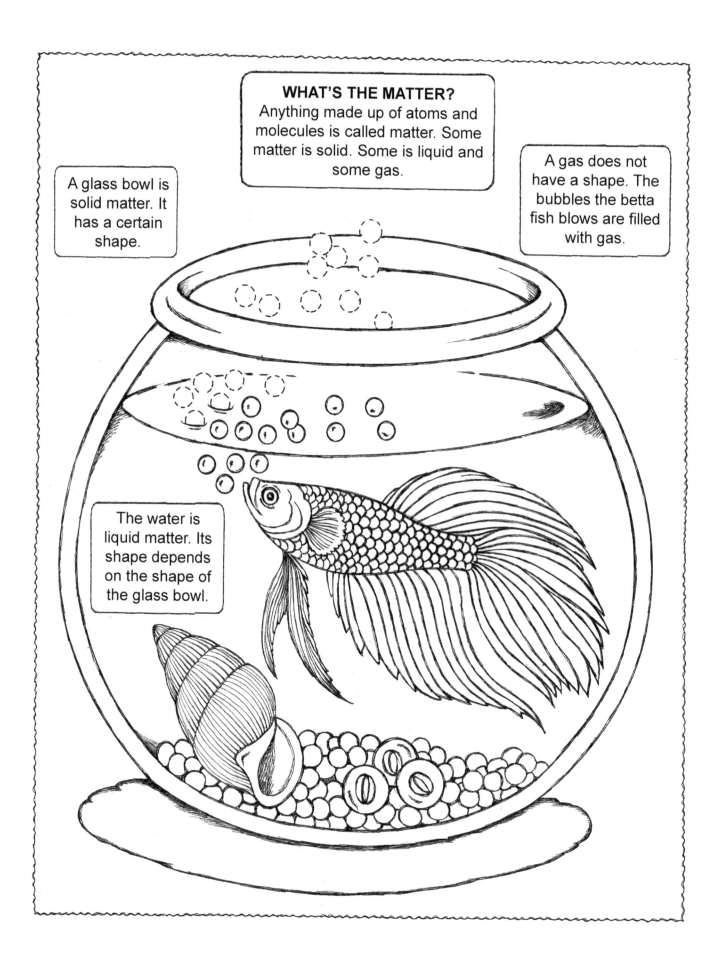

WHAT'S THE MATTER?
Anything made up of atoms and molecules is called matter. Some matter is solid. Some is liquid and some gas.

A glass bowl is solid matter. It has a certain shape.

A gas does not have a shape. The bubbles the betta fish blows are filled with gas.

The water is liquid matter. Its shape depends on the shape of the glass bowl.

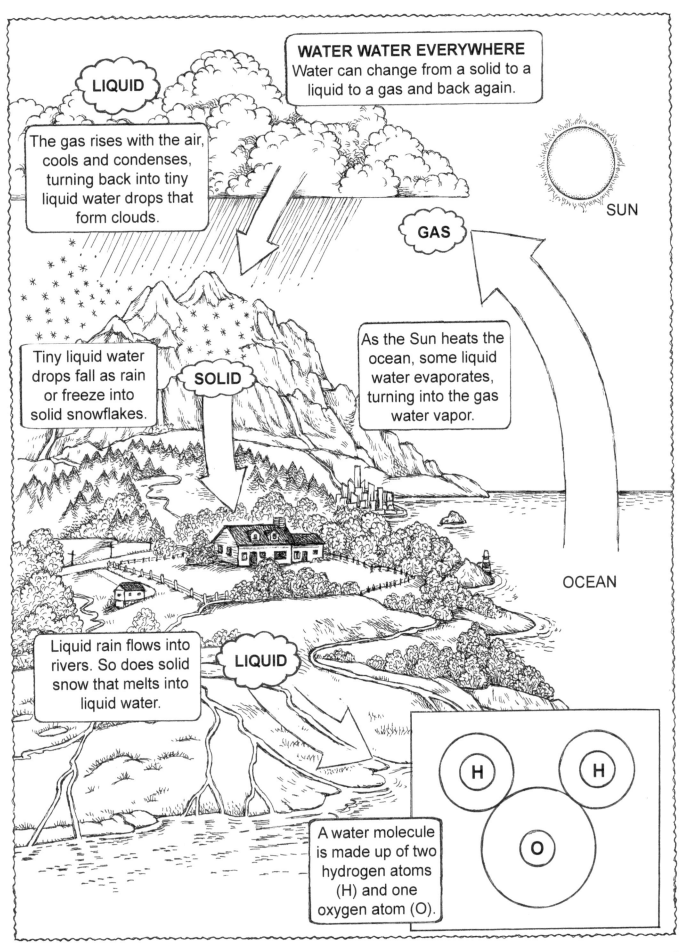

MAKING THINGS MOVE
The stone, the beetle and the yarn ball are not moving. They will not move until something pushes or pulls them. A push or a pull is a force.

A woodpecker pulls a beetle out from under the bark.

If the cat pushes a ball of yarn with its paw, the yarn will move.

A force can also change how something moves. It can make it move faster or slower or change its direction.

The pushing or pulling force of the ants is not strong enough to make the stone move.

6

MOVING SLOW, MOVING FAST
The tortoise and the hare are having a race. The hare wins because it moves faster than the slow tortoise.

How fast something moves is its speed or velocity.

How far something moves is the distance. In the race, the distance is to the finish line.

FINISH

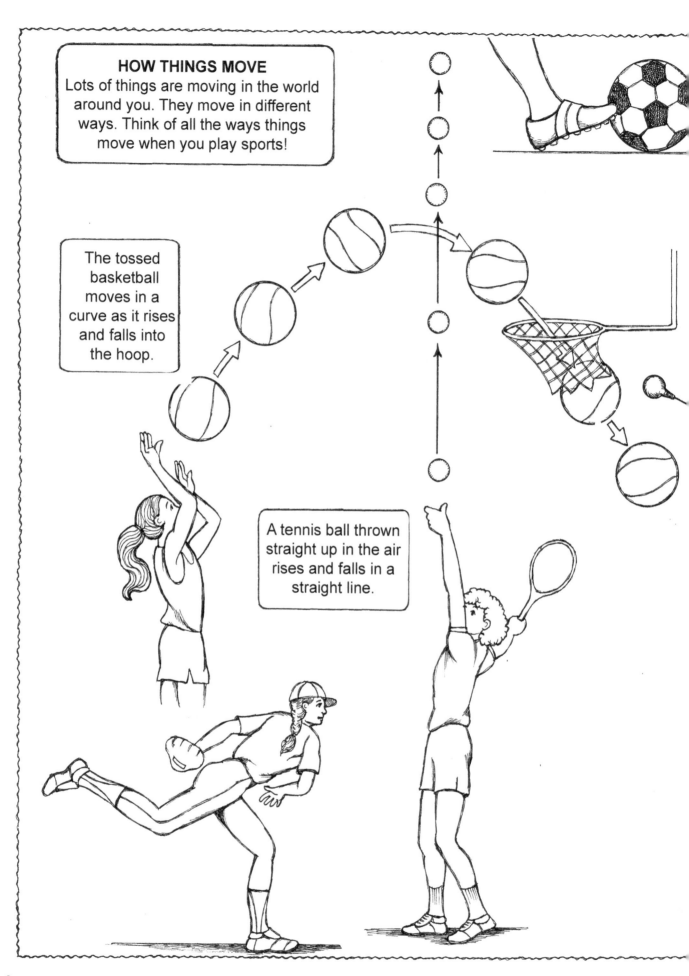

HOW THINGS MOVE
Lots of things are moving in the world around you. They move in different ways. Think of all the ways things move when you play sports!

The tossed basketball moves in a curve as it rises and falls into the hoop.

A tennis ball thrown straight up in the air rises and falls in a straight line.

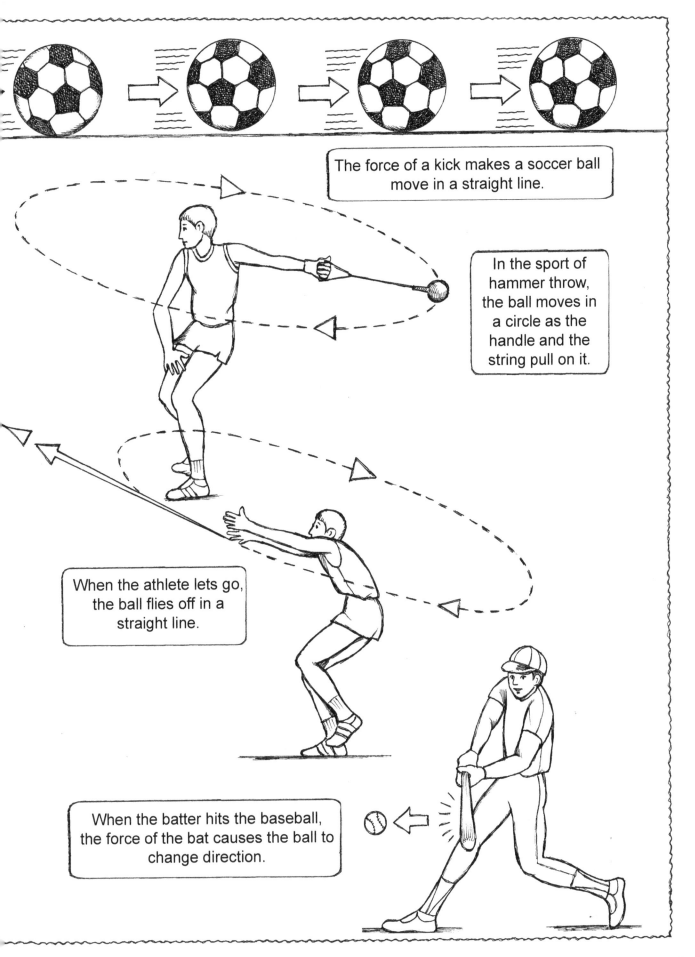

The force of a kick makes a soccer ball move in a straight line.

In the sport of hammer throw, the ball moves in a circle as the handle and the string pull on it.

When the athlete lets go, the ball flies off in a straight line.

When the batter hits the baseball, the force of the bat causes the ball to change direction.

MOVING FASTER AND FASTER
A cheetah runs faster and faster toward a zebra. This change in how fast it runs is called acceleration.

The faster the cheetah moves, the more force it has when it attacks the zebra.

A car accelerates when it goes faster. It also accelerates when it turns.

SLOWING AND STOPPING THINGS THAT MOVE
It takes a force to make things move. The force called friction can make things slow down and stop moving.

If a moving soccer ball rubs against grass, the friction caused by the rubbing slows the ball down until it stops.

Without a force like friction to stop it, the soccer ball would just keep moving in a straight line.

When a flying squirrel leaps off a high branch, it opens skin flaps that connect its legs.

As the squirrel glides along, the air pushing against the flaps slows the squirrel down.

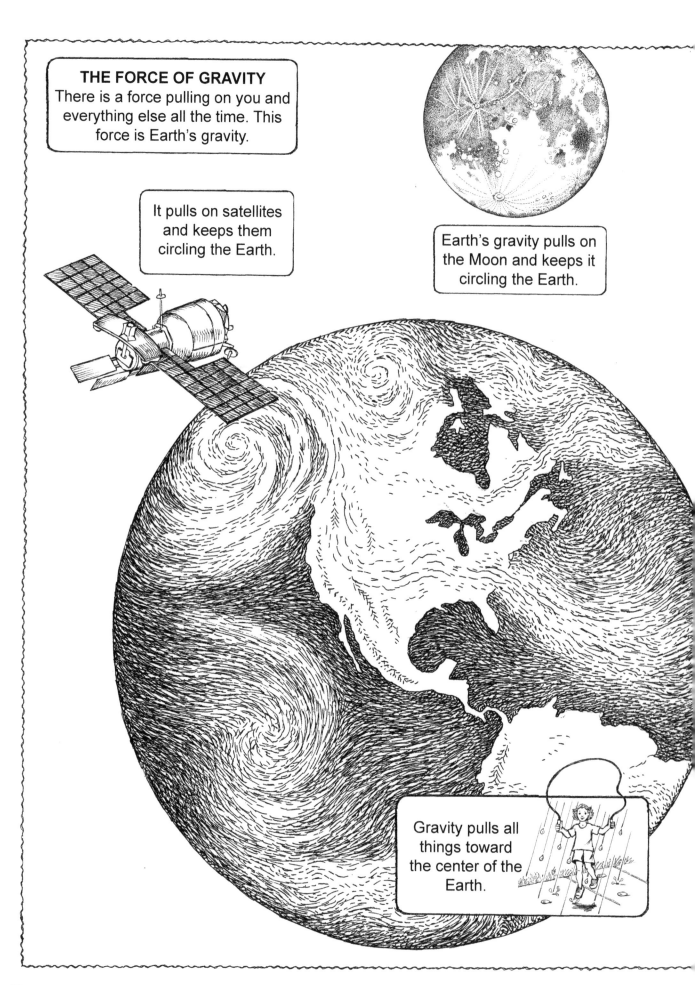

THE FORCE OF GRAVITY
There is a force pulling on you and everything else all the time. This force is Earth's gravity.

It pulls on satellites and keeps them circling the Earth.

Earth's gravity pulls on the Moon and keeps it circling the Earth.

Gravity pulls all things toward the center of the Earth.

An Egyptian vulture drops a rock to crack open the ostrich egg. Gravity pulls the rock down toward the egg and makes it fall faster and faster.

Isaac Newton discovered how the force of gravity works.

The Sun's gravity pulls on all the planets and keeps them in orbit around it.

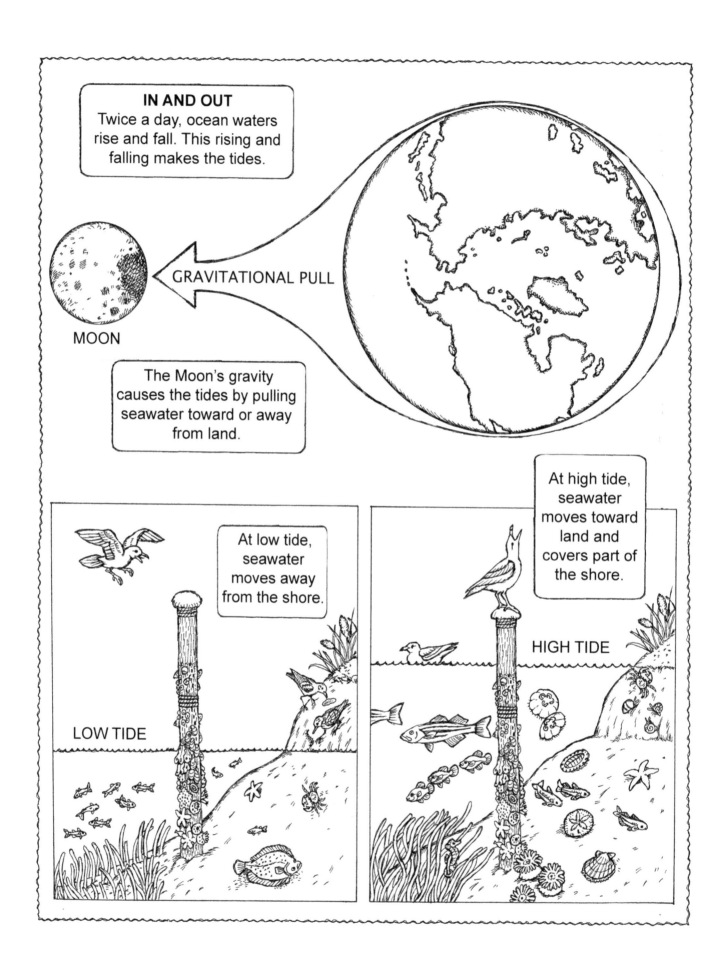

IN AND OUT
Twice a day, ocean waters rise and fall. This rising and falling makes the tides.

GRAVITATIONAL PULL

MOON

The Moon's gravity causes the tides by pulling seawater toward or away from land.

At high tide, seawater moves toward land and covers part of the shore.

At low tide, seawater moves away from the shore.

HIGH TIDE

LOW TIDE

SINK OR FLOAT
Gently drop a rubber duckie and a pebble into a pond. What happens? The duckie floats but the pebble sinks.

When they hit the water, the water moves aside to make room for each of them. The more water that moves aside, the stronger the water pushes up on them.

SWIM BLADDER

Inside the fish is a swim bladder. The swim bladder fills with gas until its body pushes aside just enough water so that the force pushing up equals the force pulling down.

The duckie floats because the force of the water pushing up on it is stronger than the force of gravity pulling it down.

The force of the water pushing up on this large ship is strong enough to keep it afloat.

PEBBLE

The pebble sinks because the force of gravity pulling it down is stronger than the force of water pushing up on it.

HOW MUCH STUFF?
The "stuff" that you and the things around you are made of is atoms and molecules. How much stuff makes up a thing is called its mass.

A blue whale has as much mass as 30 elephants.

A brick has more mass than a teddy bear. It takes more pulling force to lift a brick than to lift a teddy bear. The more mass something has, the more it weighs.

Mass tells you how strong a push or pull it takes to make something move. The more stuff a thing is made of, the more force is needed to make it move.

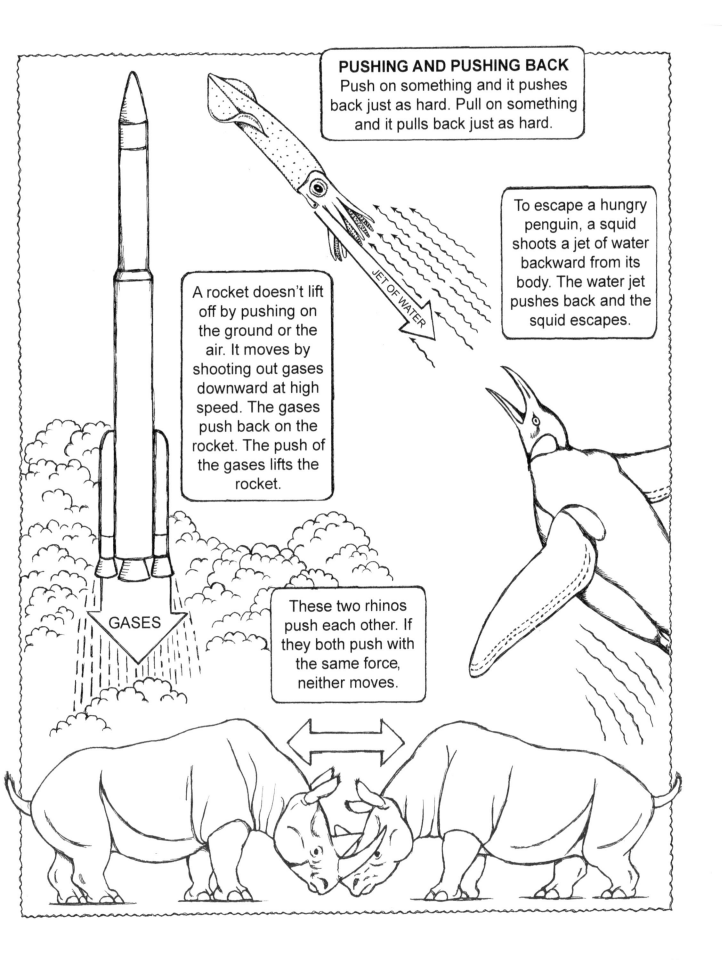

PUSHING AND PUSHING BACK
Push on something and it pushes back just as hard. Pull on something and it pulls back just as hard.

To escape a hungry penguin, a squid shoots a jet of water backward from its body. The water jet pushes back and the squid escapes.

JET OF WATER

A rocket doesn't lift off by pushing on the ground or the air. It moves by shooting out gases downward at high speed. The gases push back on the rocket. The push of the gases lifts the rocket.

GASES

These two rhinos push each other. If they both push with the same force, neither moves.

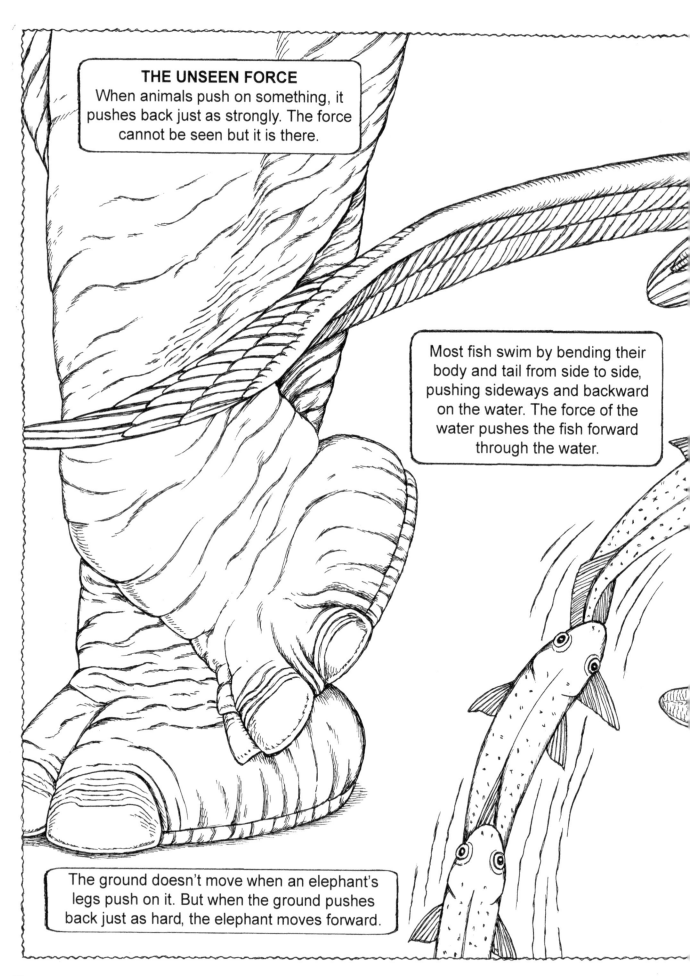

THE UNSEEN FORCE
When animals push on something, it pushes back just as strongly. The force cannot be seen but it is there.

Most fish swim by bending their body and tail from side to side, pushing sideways and backward on the water. The force of the water pushes the fish forward through the water.

The ground doesn't move when an elephant's legs push on it. But when the ground pushes back just as hard, the elephant moves forward.

When an albatross flaps its wings it pushes air downward and backward. The air pushes back on the bird, lifting it and moving it forward.

When the grasshopper's legs push back on the hoe, the hoe doesn't move. Instead, the hoe pushes back just as hard and the grasshopper leaps into the air.

To slither forward, this snake pushes off the ground, which pushes back on it.

When a beaver's large webbed feet push water backward, the water pushes the beaver forward as it swims.

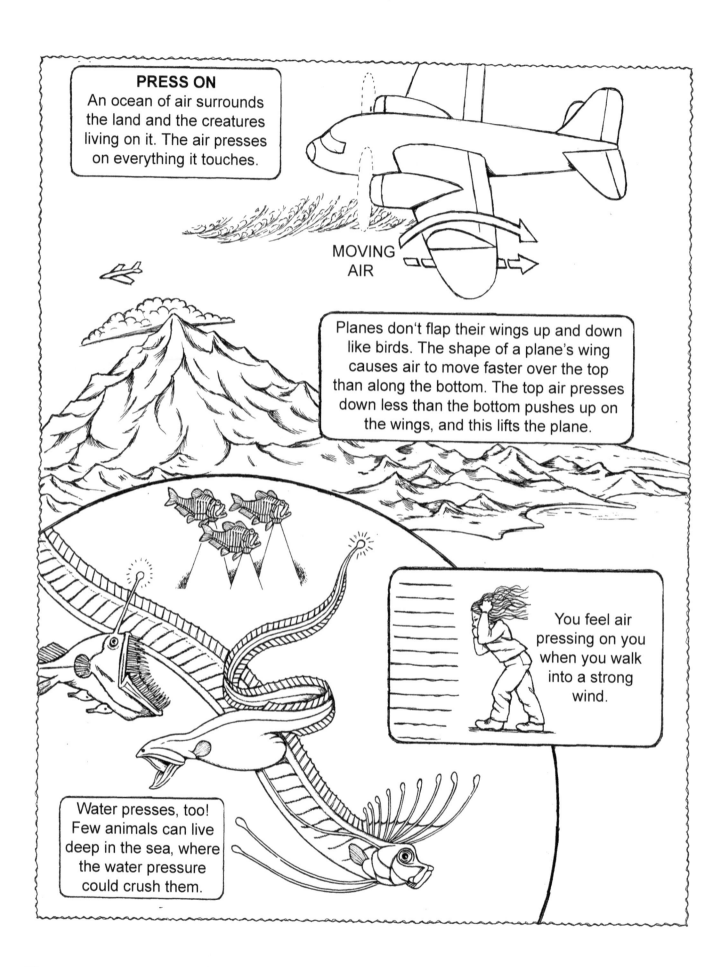

PRESS ON
An ocean of air surrounds the land and the creatures living on it. The air presses on everything it touches.

MOVING AIR

Planes don't flap their wings up and down like birds. The shape of a plane's wing causes air to move faster over the top than along the bottom. The top air presses down less than the bottom pushes up on the wings, and this lifts the plane.

You feel air pressing on you when you walk into a strong wind.

Water presses, too! Few animals can live deep in the sea, where the water pressure could crush them.

20

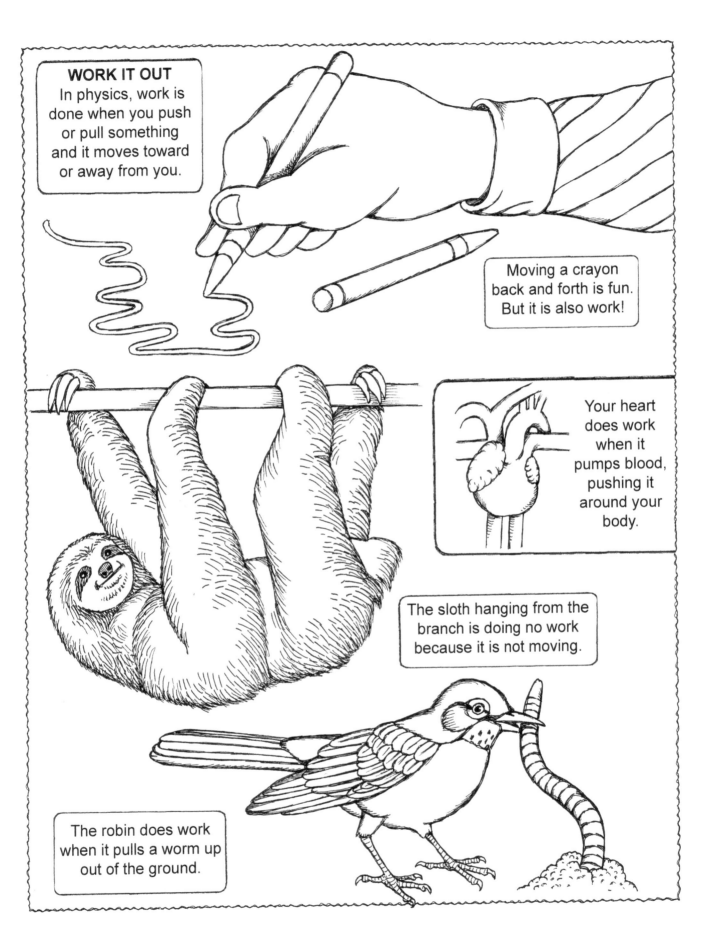

WORK IT OUT
In physics, work is done when you push or pull something and it moves toward or away from you.

Moving a crayon back and forth is fun. But it is also work!

Your heart does work when it pumps blood, pushing it around your body.

The sloth hanging from the branch is doing no work because it is not moving.

The robin does work when it pulls a worm up out of the ground.

LEVER

EASY DOES IT
Machines make it easier to do work. They can help get the job done with less pushing or pulling.

A lever is a long rod used to lift something heavy with less force.

It is easier for a person to slide a piano up a ramp than to lift it.

RAMP

A wedge is used to split something apart.

PULLEY

It is easier to pull down on the pulley's rope than to pull up on the heavy weight.

WEDGE

100

23

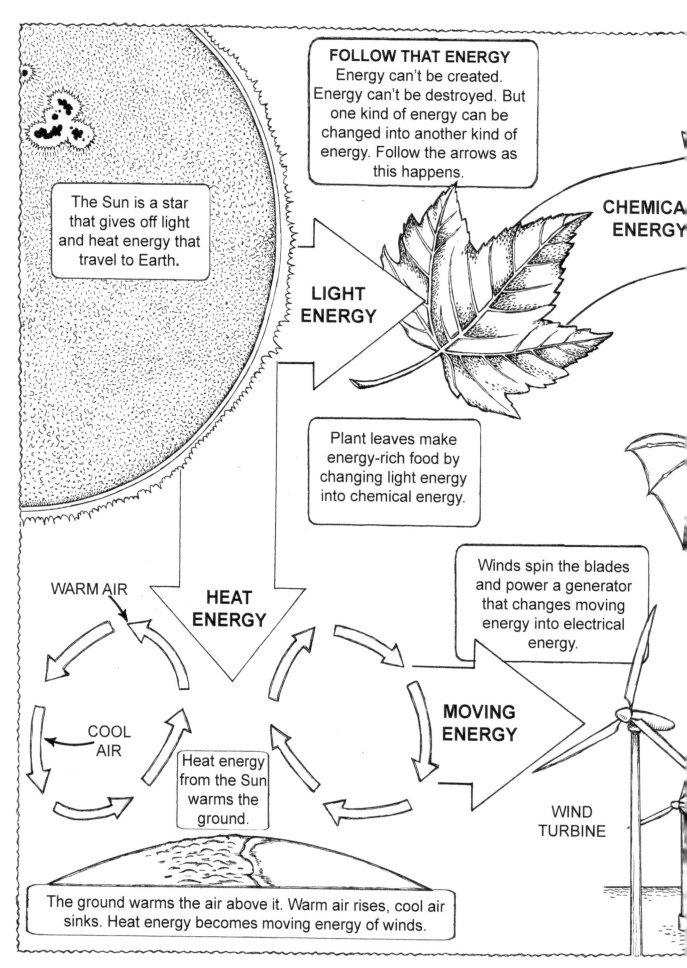

FOLLOW THAT ENERGY
Energy can't be created. Energy can't be destroyed. But one kind of energy can be changed into another kind of energy. Follow the arrows as this happens.

The Sun is a star that gives off light and heat energy that travel to Earth.

CHEMICAL ENERGY

LIGHT ENERGY

Plant leaves make energy-rich food by changing light energy into chemical energy.

HEAT ENERGY

WARM AIR

COOL AIR

Heat energy from the Sun warms the ground.

Winds spin the blades and power a generator that changes moving energy into electrical energy.

MOVING ENERGY

WIND TURBINE

The ground warms the air above it. Warm air rises, cool air sinks. Heat energy becomes moving energy of winds.

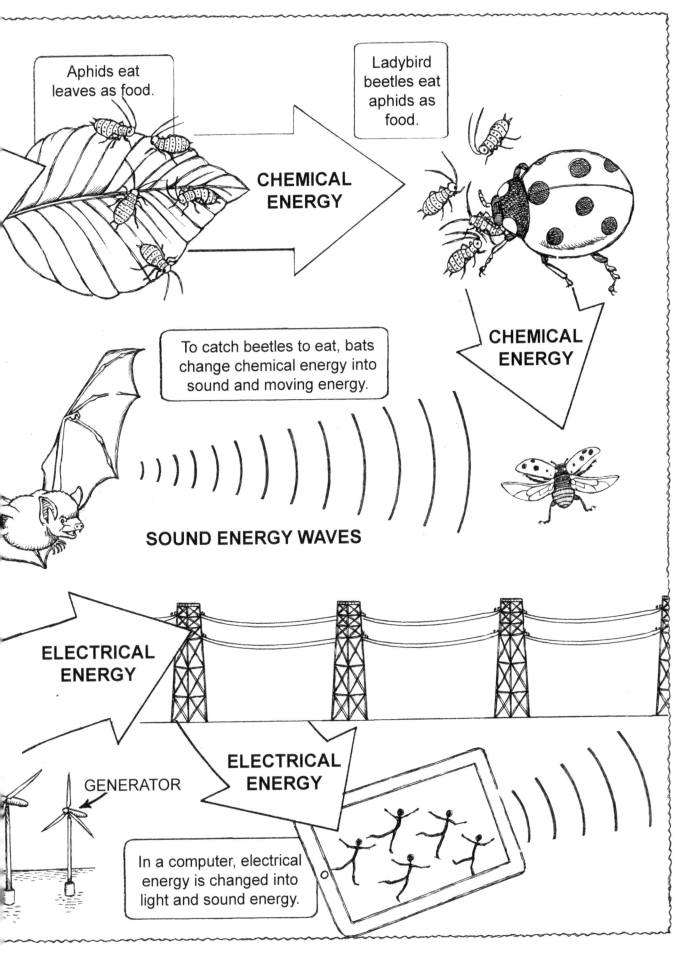

Aphids eat leaves as food.

Ladybird beetles eat aphids as food.

CHEMICAL ENERGY

CHEMICAL ENERGY

To catch beetles to eat, bats change chemical energy into sound and moving energy.

SOUND ENERGY WAVES

ELECTRICAL ENERGY

ELECTRICAL ENERGY

GENERATOR

In a computer, electrical energy is changed into light and sound energy.

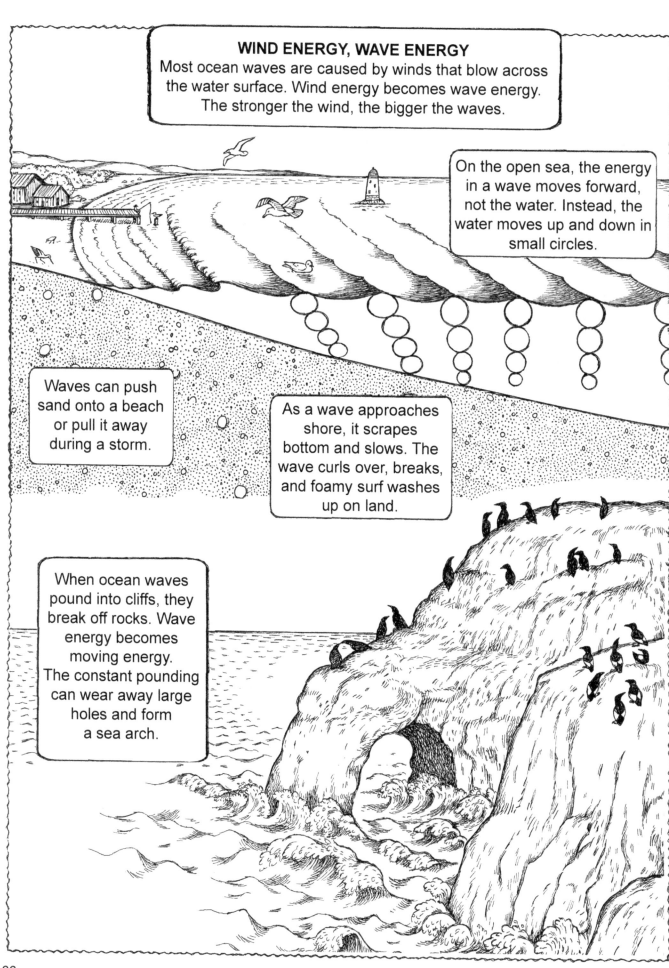

WIND ENERGY, WAVE ENERGY
Most ocean waves are caused by winds that blow across the water surface. Wind energy becomes wave energy. The stronger the wind, the bigger the waves.

On the open sea, the energy in a wave moves forward, not the water. Instead, the water moves up and down in small circles.

Waves can push sand onto a beach or pull it away during a storm.

As a wave approaches shore, it scrapes bottom and slows. The wave curls over, breaks, and foamy surf washes up on land.

When ocean waves pound into cliffs, they break off rocks. Wave energy becomes moving energy. The constant pounding can wear away large holes and form a sea arch.

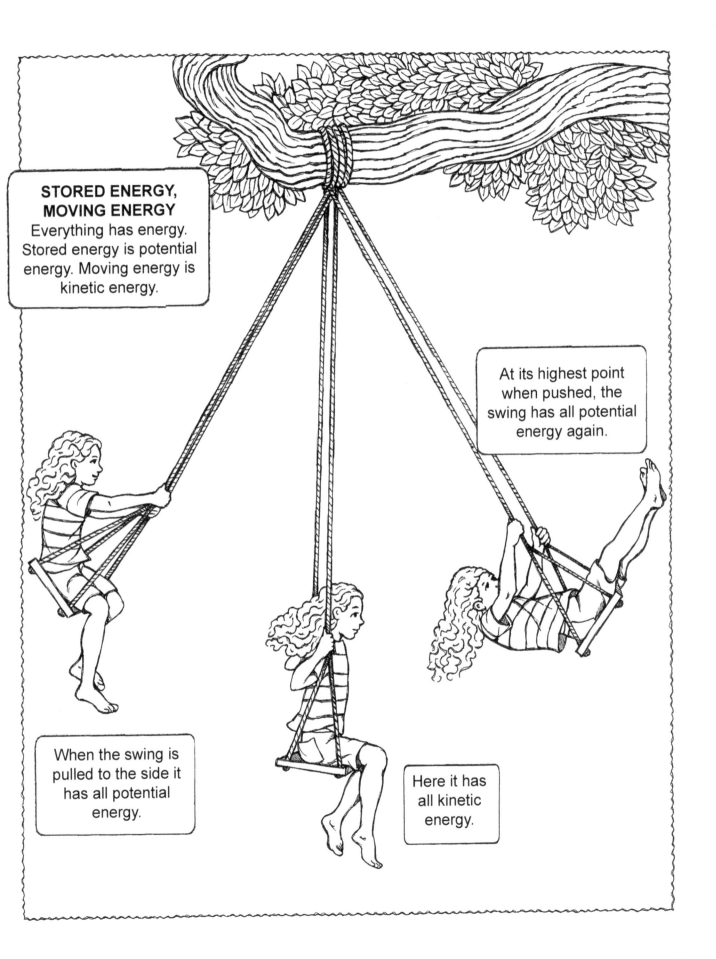

STORED ENERGY, MOVING ENERGY
Everything has energy. Stored energy is potential energy. Moving energy is kinetic energy.

At its highest point when pushed, the swing has all potential energy again.

When the swing is pulled to the side it has all potential energy.

Here it has all kinetic energy.

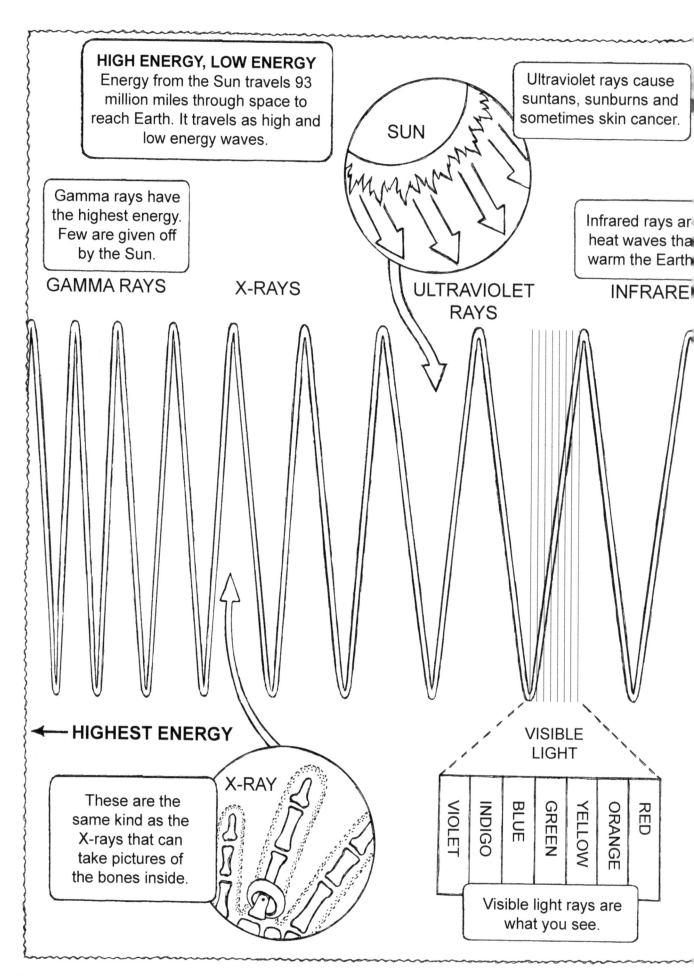

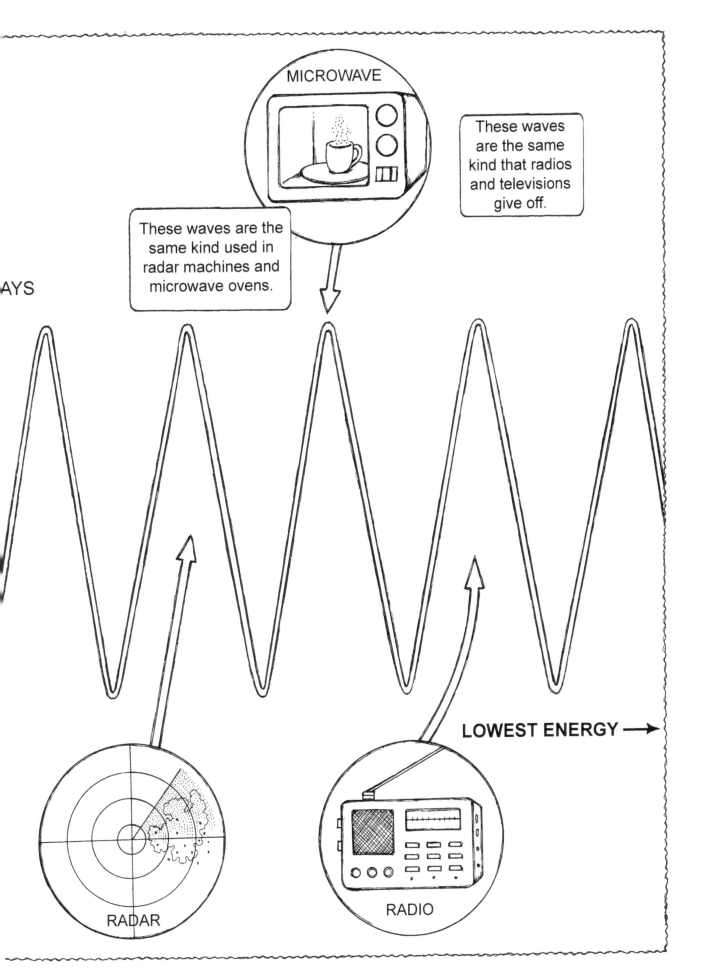

ALL ABOUT LIGHT
Light is a kind of energy. Some light waves you can see. Others you cannot.

When sunlight hits falling raindrops, they can act like prisms and form a rainbow.

RED
ORANGE
YELLOW
GREEN
BLUE
INDIGO
VIOLET

Light travels faster than anything else. It speeds along at 186,000 miles every second.

White light is a mix of all colors. When white light hits a red flower, the petals soak up all colors except red. You see red light waves bouncing back to your eyes.

When light waves pass through a prism, they slow down, bend, and separate into colors.

WHITE LIGHT

RED
ORANGE
YELLOW
GREEN
BLUE
INDIGO
VIOLET

NIGHT LIGHT
Like the Sun, all the other stars in the night sky give off light. The Moon, however, does not make its own light. Instead, it reflects light from the Sun.

In a light bulb, electrical energy is changed into light energy.

When light bounces off the back of a fox's eyes, they seem to glow. The reflected light helps the fox see in the dark.

Fireflies can change chemical energy into light energy and glow in the darkness.

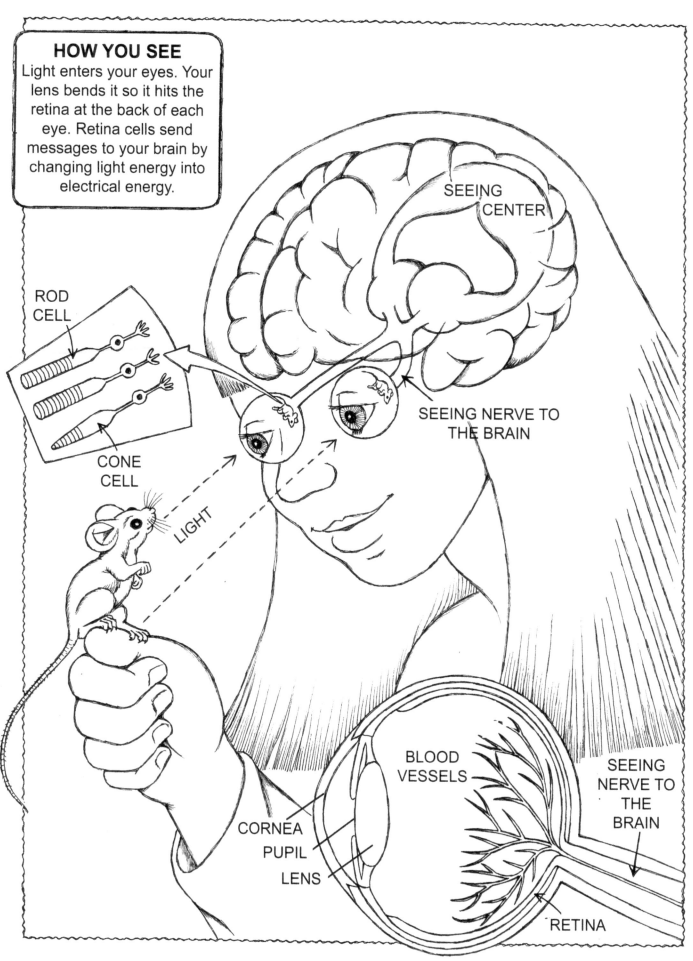

HOW YOU SEE
Light enters your eyes. Your lens bends it so it hits the retina at the back of each eye. Retina cells send messages to your brain by changing light energy into electrical energy.

SEEING CENTER

ROD CELL

CONE CELL

SEEING NERVE TO THE BRAIN

LIGHT

BLOOD VESSELS

SEEING NERVE TO THE BRAIN

CORNEA
PUPIL
LENS

RETINA

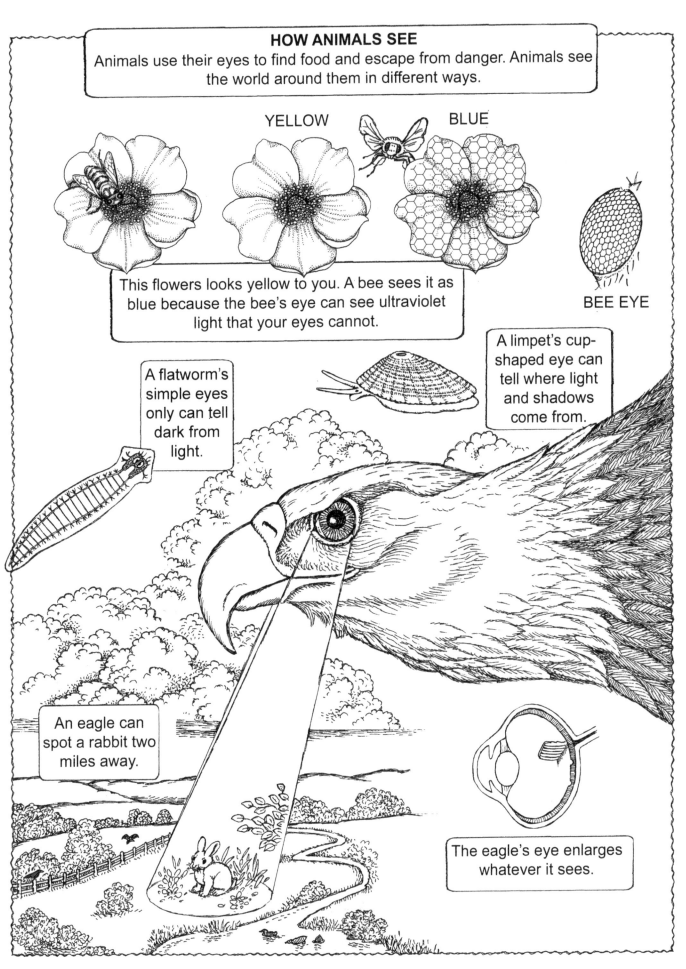

HOW ANIMALS SEE
Animals use their eyes to find food and escape from danger. Animals see the world around them in different ways.

YELLOW

BLUE

This flowers looks yellow to you. A bee sees it as blue because the bee's eye can see ultraviolet light that your eyes cannot.

BEE EYE

A flatworm's simple eyes only can tell dark from light.

A limpet's cup-shaped eye can tell where light and shadows come from.

An eagle can spot a rabbit two miles away.

The eagle's eye enlarges whatever it sees.

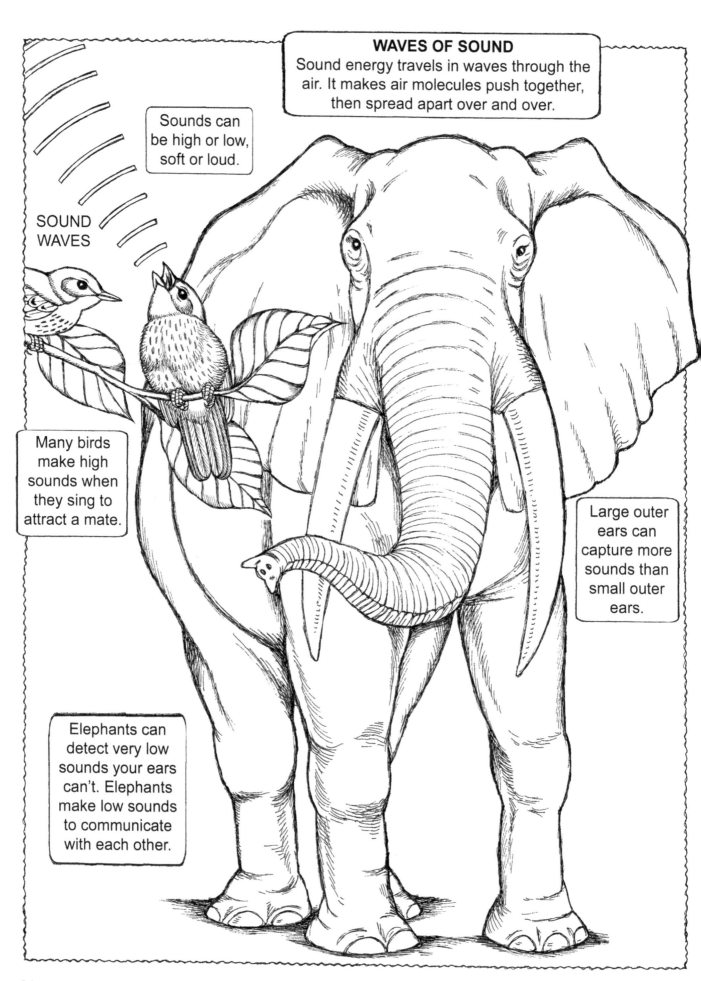

WAVES OF SOUND
Sound energy travels in waves through the air. It makes air molecules push together, then spread apart over and over.

Sounds can be high or low, soft or loud.

SOUND WAVES

Many birds make high sounds when they sing to attract a mate.

Large outer ears can capture more sounds than small outer ears.

Elephants can detect very low sounds your ears can't. Elephants make low sounds to communicate with each other.

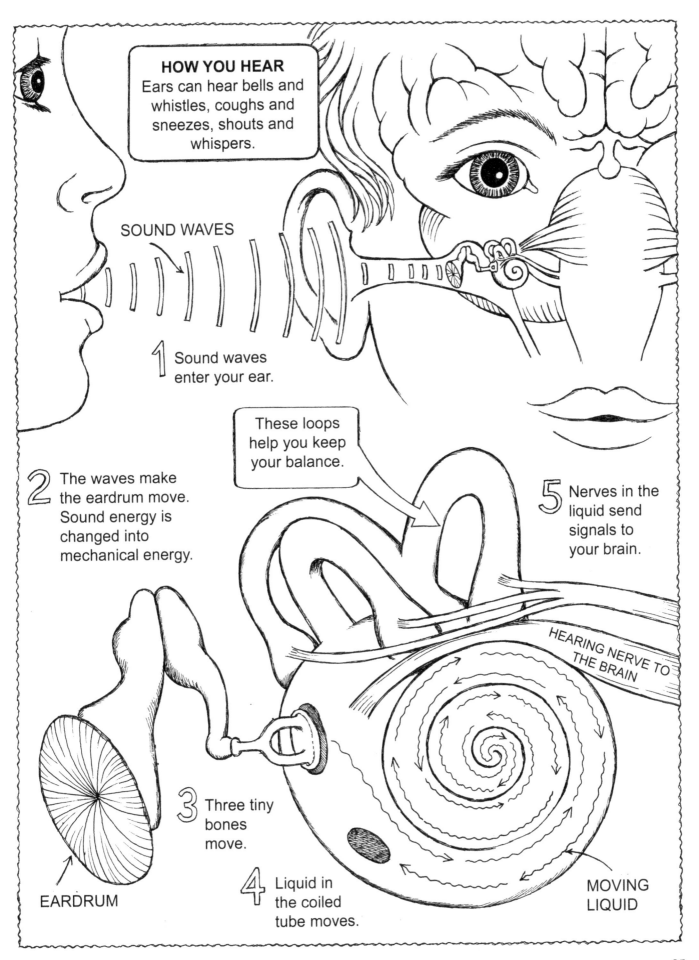

HOW YOU HEAR
Ears can hear bells and whistles, coughs and sneezes, shouts and whispers.

SOUND WAVES

1 Sound waves enter your ear.

These loops help you keep your balance.

2 The waves make the eardrum move. Sound energy is changed into mechanical energy.

5 Nerves in the liquid send signals to your brain.

HEARING NERVE TO THE BRAIN

3 Three tiny bones move.

4 Liquid in the coiled tube moves.

EARDRUM

MOVING LIQUID

35

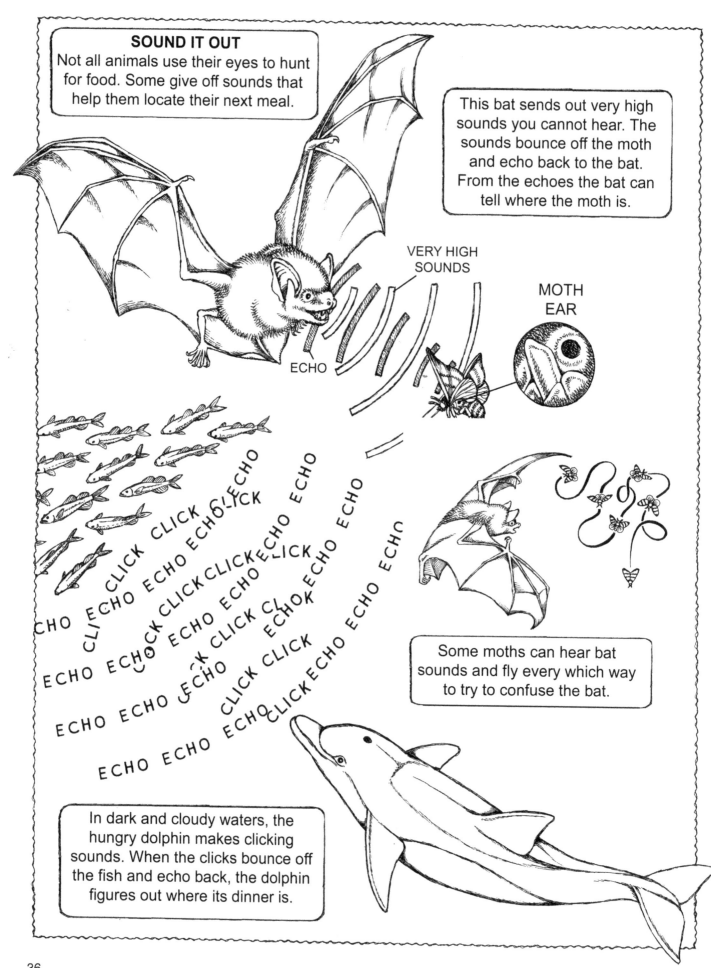

SOUND IT OUT
Not all animals use their eyes to hunt for food. Some give off sounds that help them locate their next meal.

This bat sends out very high sounds you cannot hear. The sounds bounce off the moth and echo back to the bat. From the echoes the bat can tell where the moth is.

VERY HIGH SOUNDS

MOTH EAR

ECHO

Some moths can hear bat sounds and fly every which way to try to confuse the bat.

CLICK CLICK CLICK ECHO ECHO ECHO CLICK CLICK CLICK ECHO ECHO ECHO CLICK ECHO ECHO ECHO ECHO CLICK CLICK ECHO ECHO CLICK CLICK ECHO ECHO ECHO CLICK CLICK ECHO ECHO ECHO ECHO ECHO ECHO CLICK CLICK ECHO ECHO ECHO

In dark and cloudy waters, the hungry dolphin makes clicking sounds. When the clicks bounce off the fish and echo back, the dolphin figures out where its dinner is.

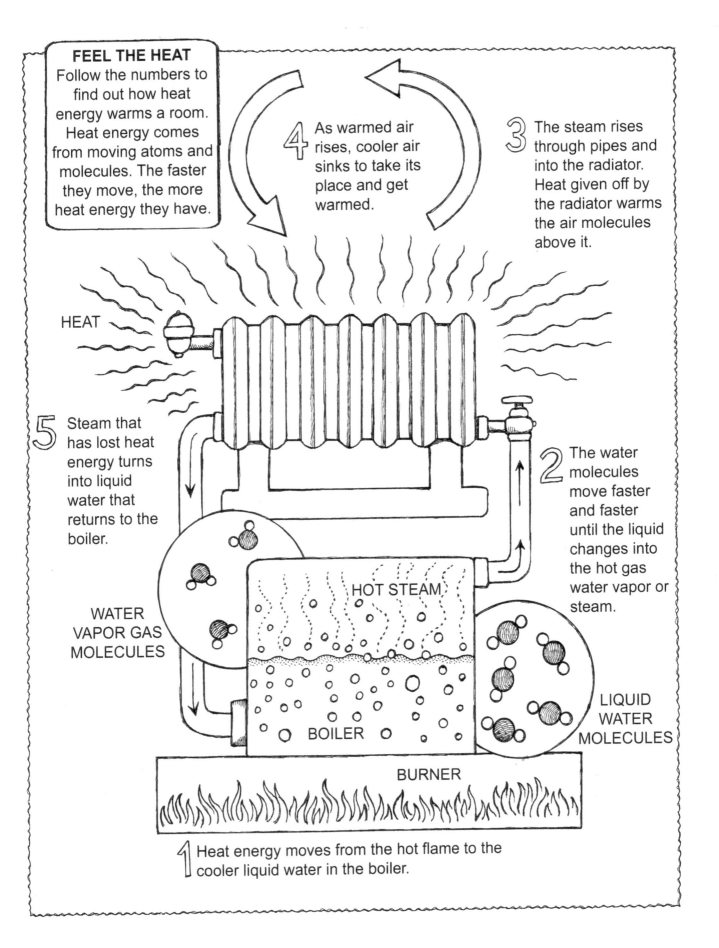

FEEL THE HEAT
Follow the numbers to find out how heat energy warms a room. Heat energy comes from moving atoms and molecules. The faster they move, the more heat energy they have.

4 As warmed air rises, cooler air sinks to take its place and get warmed.

3 The steam rises through pipes and into the radiator. Heat given off by the radiator warms the air molecules above it.

HEAT

5 Steam that has lost heat energy turns into liquid water that returns to the boiler.

2 The water molecules move faster and faster until the liquid changes into the hot gas water vapor or steam.

WATER VAPOR GAS MOLECULES

HOT STEAM

LIQUID WATER MOLECULES

BOILER

BURNER

1 Heat energy moves from the hot flame to the cooler liquid water in the boiler.

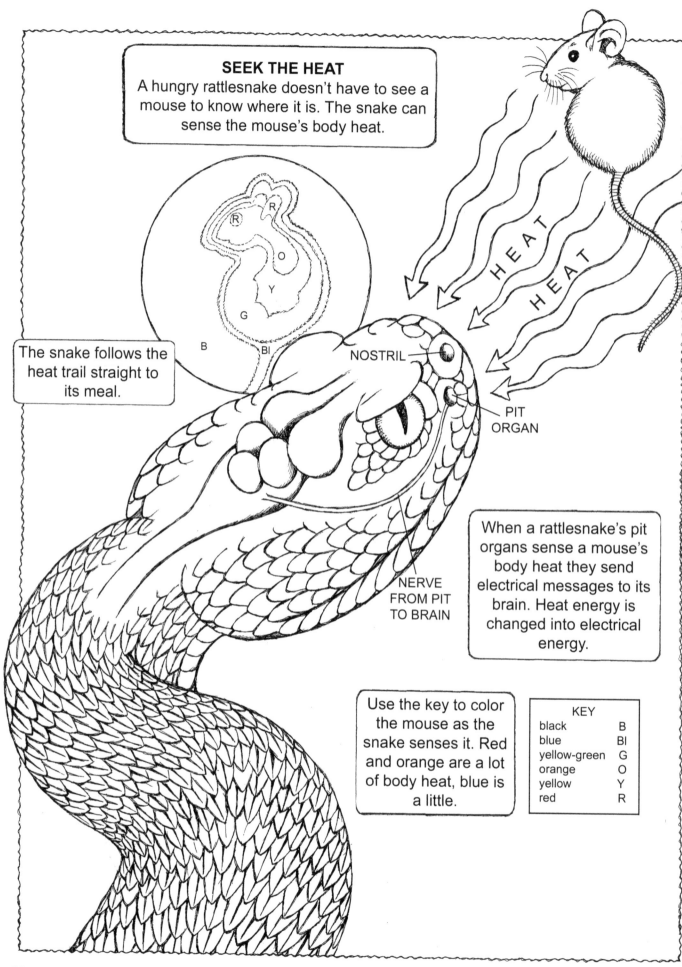

SEEK THE HEAT
A hungry rattlesnake doesn't have to see a mouse to know where it is. The snake can sense the mouse's body heat.

The snake follows the heat trail straight to its meal.

HEAT

HEAT

NOSTRIL

PIT ORGAN

NERVE FROM PIT TO BRAIN

When a rattlesnake's pit organs sense a mouse's body heat they send electrical messages to its brain. Heat energy is changed into electrical energy.

Use the key to color the mouse as the snake senses it. Red and orange are a lot of body heat, blue is a little.

KEY	
black	B
blue	Bl
yellow-green	G
orange	O
yellow	Y
red	R

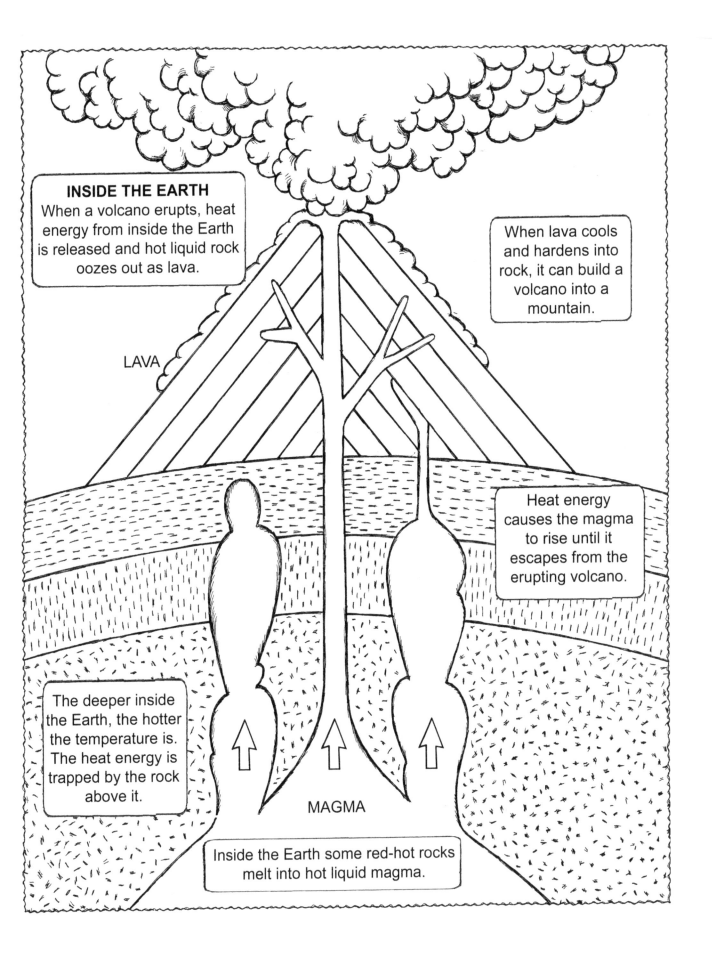

INSIDE THE EARTH
When a volcano erupts, heat energy from inside the Earth is released and hot liquid rock oozes out as lava.

When lava cools and hardens into rock, it can build a volcano into a mountain.

LAVA

Heat energy causes the magma to rise until it escapes from the erupting volcano.

The deeper inside the Earth, the hotter the temperature is. The heat energy is trapped by the rock above it.

MAGMA

Inside the Earth some red-hot rocks melt into hot liquid magma.

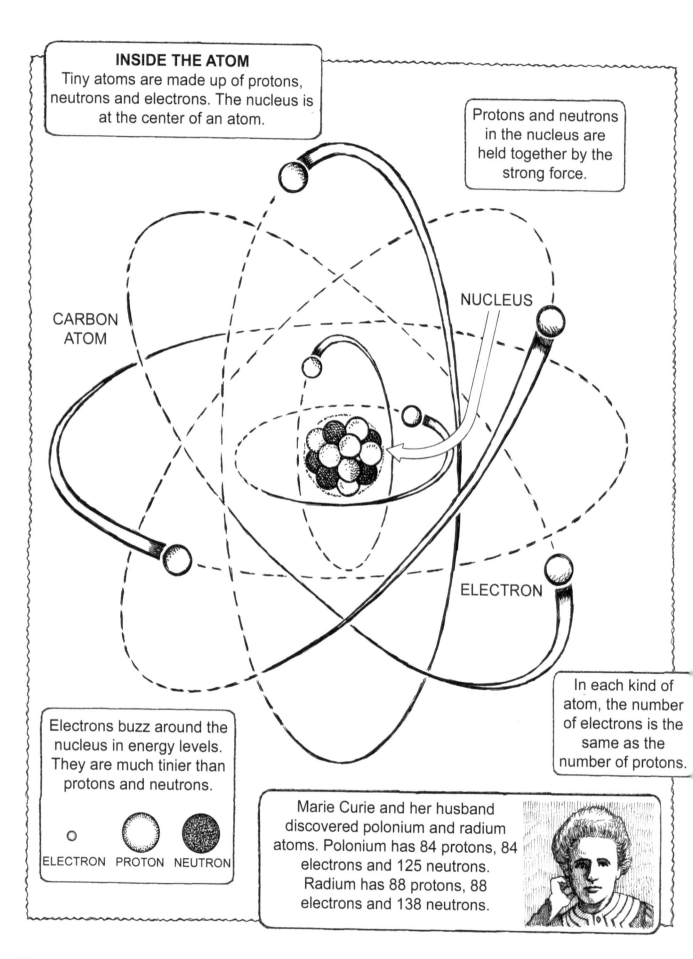

INSIDE THE ATOM
Tiny atoms are made up of protons, neutrons and electrons. The nucleus is at the center of an atom.

Protons and neutrons in the nucleus are held together by the strong force.

NUCLEUS

CARBON ATOM

ELECTRON

In each kind of atom, the number of electrons is the same as the number of protons.

Electrons buzz around the nucleus in energy levels. They are much tinier than protons and neutrons.

ELECTRON   PROTON   NEUTRON

Marie Curie and her husband discovered polonium and radium atoms. Polonium has 84 protons, 84 electrons and 125 neutrons. Radium has 88 protons, 88 electrons and 138 neutrons.

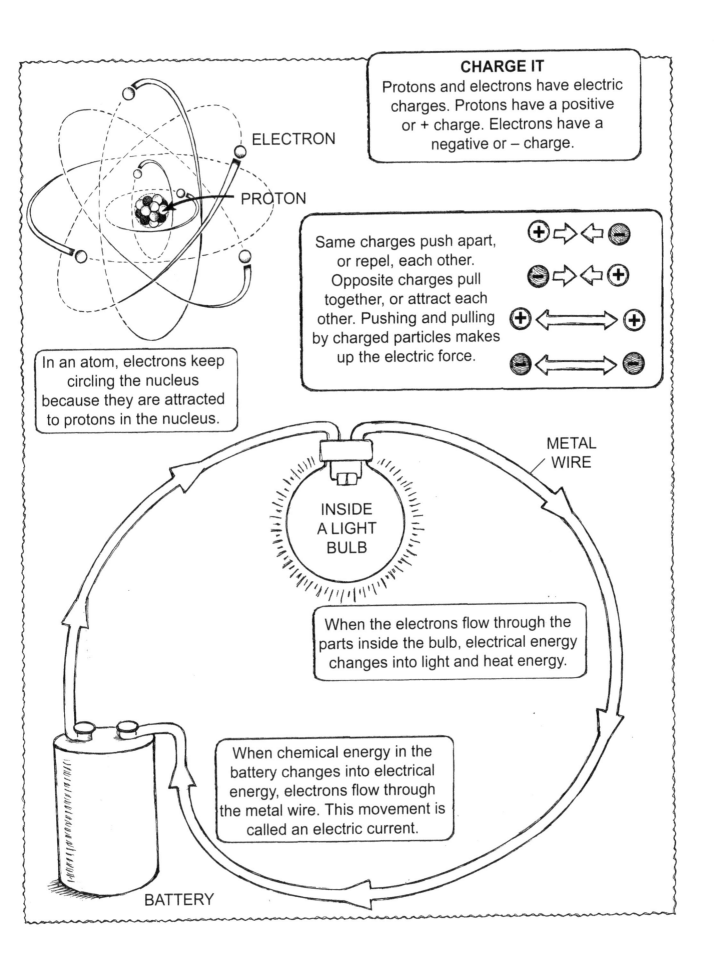

ELECTRON

PROTON

CHARGE IT
Protons and electrons have electric charges. Protons have a positive or + charge. Electrons have a negative or – charge.

In an atom, electrons keep circling the nucleus because they are attracted to protons in the nucleus.

Same charges push apart, or repel, each other. Opposite charges pull together, or attract each other. Pushing and pulling by charged particles makes up the electric force.

METAL WIRE

INSIDE A LIGHT BULB

When the electrons flow through the parts inside the bulb, electrical energy changes into light and heat energy.

When chemical energy in the battery changes into electrical energy, electrons flow through the metal wire. This movement is called an electric current.

BATTERY

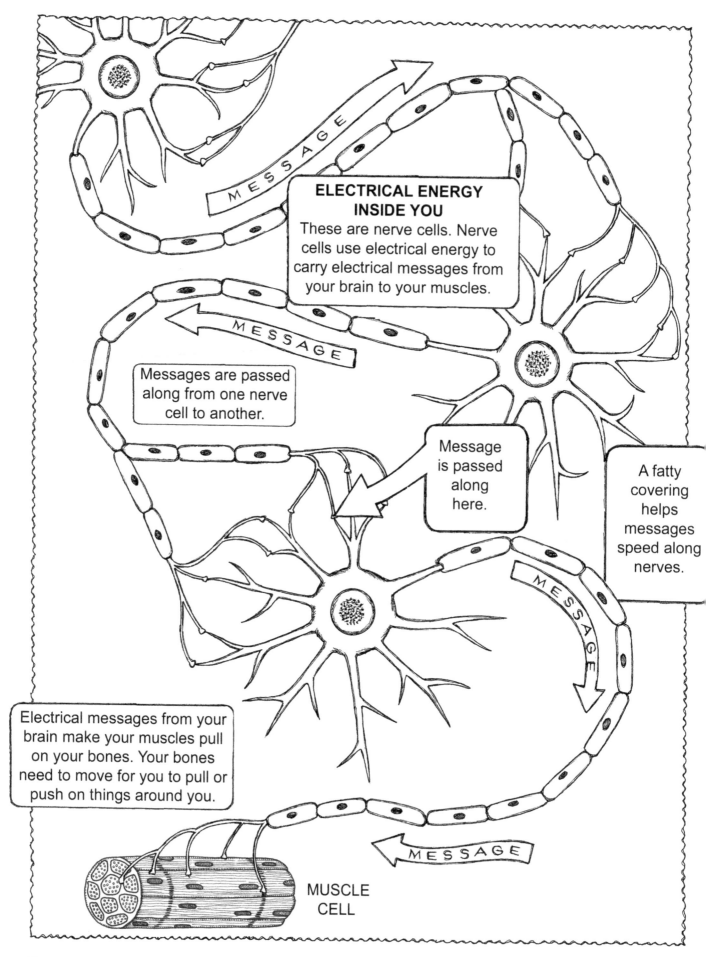

ELECTRICAL ENERGY INSIDE YOU
These are nerve cells. Nerve cells use electrical energy to carry electrical messages from your brain to your muscles.

Messages are passed along from one nerve cell to another.

Message is passed along here.

A fatty covering helps messages speed along nerves.

Electrical messages from your brain make your muscles pull on your bones. Your bones need to move for you to pull or push on things around you.

MUSCLE CELL

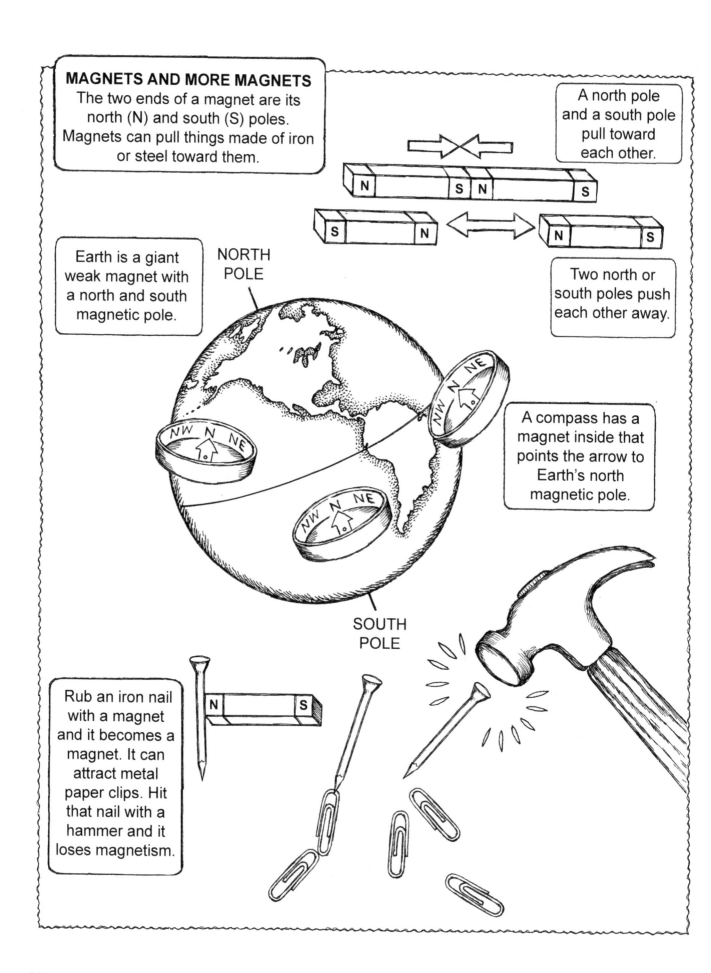

MAGNETS AND MORE MAGNETS
The two ends of a magnet are its north (N) and south (S) poles. Magnets can pull things made of iron or steel toward them.

A north pole and a south pole pull toward each other.

Two north or south poles push each other away.

Earth is a giant weak magnet with a north and south magnetic pole.

NORTH POLE

A compass has a magnet inside that points the arrow to Earth's north magnetic pole.

SOUTH POLE

Rub an iron nail with a magnet and it becomes a magnet. It can attract metal paper clips. Hit that nail with a hammer and it loses magnetism.

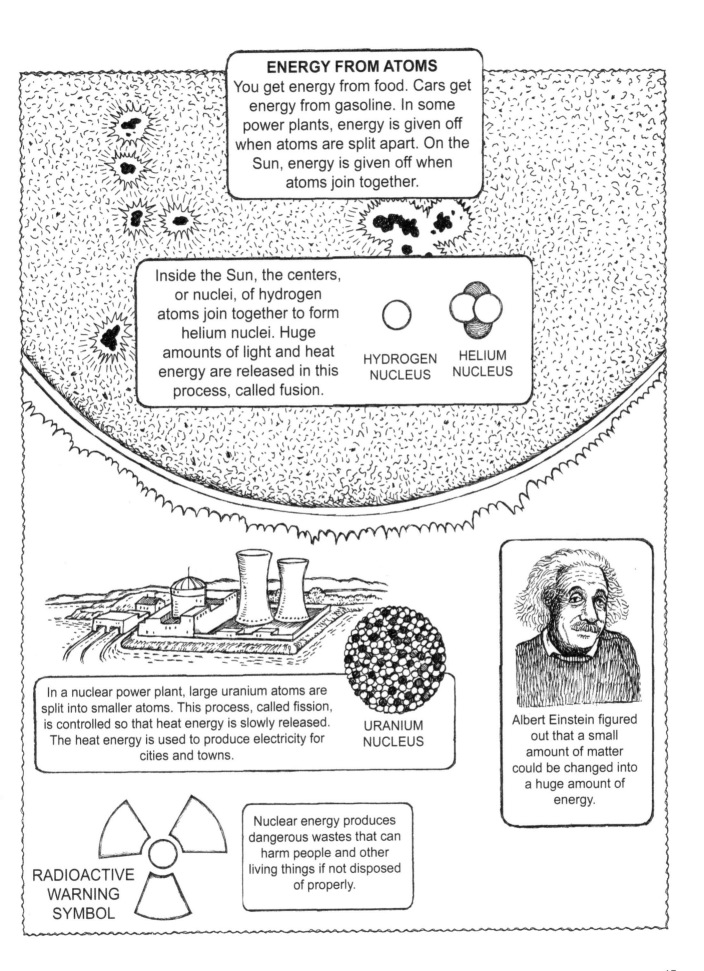

ENERGY FROM ATOMS

You get energy from food. Cars get energy from gasoline. In some power plants, energy is given off when atoms are split apart. On the Sun, energy is given off when atoms join together.

Inside the Sun, the centers, or nuclei, of hydrogen atoms join together to form helium nuclei. Huge amounts of light and heat energy are released in this process, called fusion.

HYDROGEN NUCLEUS

HELIUM NUCLEUS

In a nuclear power plant, large uranium atoms are split into smaller atoms. This process, called fission, is controlled so that heat energy is slowly released. The heat energy is used to produce electricity for cities and towns.

URANIUM NUCLEUS

Albert Einstein figured out that a small amount of matter could be changed into a huge amount of energy.

RADIOACTIVE WARNING SYMBOL

Nuclear energy produces dangerous wastes that can harm people and other living things if not disposed of properly.